CONFIDENCE

Sell Yourself in
Medical Interviews

Jane Anderson

"Jane is absolutely amazing and I highly recommend her services. This was the first year that I was offered an interview for the highly competitive dermatology program. After five years of trying, I was keen to get on. Before the interview training, I was nervous, flustered and awkward, and had a strange and nervous tone to my voice. After one session with Jane, I was confident and able to sell myself. After my first session, I continued to practice with my husband, who was shocked at the difference and made the comment: 'Wow, you sound like a power woman!' I recently found out that I got onto the program and I am sure I would not have been able to without my interview training sessions with Jane. I have used my new-found skills in my career. I am more aware of how to put my best foot forward, and how to sell myself in what I say and how I dress. I have already noticed a difference in the way patients treat me and respond to me based on the way I present myself, the way I highlight my skills and what I wear. I can't stop raving about my experiences with Jane and I have even given my mum and dad a copy of her book (which I read from front to back). I think everyone is getting sick of me saying, 'Jane says …' Thank you once again, Jane!"
– *EP, Dermatologist, Brisbane*

"Before working with Jane, I didn't realise my potential. The sessions helped me to unleash the best in me."
– *KN, Cosmetic Surgery*

"Before working with Jane, I was an absolute mess. I had sat an interview the previous year for the training program and had done terribly. As a result, I had absolutely no confidence in my interview techniques or capabilities. After working with Jane, I was focused and driven. I knew what I needed to do to achieve my goal. I was able to shift my mindset and develop the confidence to know that I was the right fit for the program (and

show the panel that, too!). It still involved a lot of hard work but Jane was there every step of the way. I definitely would not have been able to do this without Jane's guidance and support!"
– *Melissa, Obstetrics and Gynaecology*

"Dear Jane. This is just to say a big thank you for your incredibly helpful interview skills training session earlier this year. As you know, I had an unsuccessful interview last year, so I was extremely nervous and anxious about undergoing the process again. However, when I had my interview in August, I was calm, confident and felt that I presented myself to the interview panel to the very best of my ability – and I just found out that my application for the dermatology program was a success! I know that I wouldn't have been able to achieve this without your guidance. Thank you so much for your coaching session. It is literally responsible for turning my dream job into a reality and I can't thank you enough! I will definitely recommend your interview skills training to all the other budding dermatologists!"
– *Laura, Dermatologist, Brisbane*

"Hi Jane! I got in to Derm! Thank you so, so much for all your help and wise advice. Happy to help out with any future candidates if you ever need anything. Thanks again!"
– *NW, Dermatologist, Brisbane*

"Dear Jane. I wanted to let you know that I got offered a Derm. reg. job! Woo hoo! I am so excited and happy! Thanks for all your help with preparing for the interview."
– *LB, Dermatologist, Brisbane*

"Hi Jane. Many thanks for your help with my interview preparation. I am pleased to say that I got the job! Your help was invaluable for providing me with a structure for dealing

with behavioural questions (of which there were many!) and to give me the confidence to know that I was heading in the right direction. Thanks again and I'll be sure to give your details to my colleagues in the future."
– *Ian, Urology Interview Training, Brisbane*

"Good news, the professor rang me personally last night and I have been accepted to start the training program!"
– *Chris, Periodontics Interview Training, Brisbane*

ABOUT THE AUTHOR

Jane Anderson is a communications expert in high-impact communication. She speaks, runs workshops and mentors her clients to get cut-through to their audiences faster.

She works with doctors, executives and organisation across Australia and internationally. Jane's early career involved working in marketing and human resources, building competency guides and training panels how to recruit experts in their field.

Jane has worked with more than 14,000 people on their communication skills. She is a certified Master Career Director and Executive Coach. She has written four books on high-impact communication, for both face-to-face an online. She has been featured in *The Age*, *Sydney Morning Herald*, *Marie Claire*, *Business Insider* and on Channel 9.

She is the host of the "Brand You Show" podcast, downloaded by more than 40,000 people across 80 countries, and has been nominated for the Telstra Business Women's Awards in 2014 and 2016.

Jane is based in Brisbane, Queensland, and enjoys the beach, catching up with family and spoiling her nieces and nephew.

To find out more about Jane and her programs, go to www.jane-anderson.com

CONTENTS

INTRODUCTION

I grew up and went to school in Lismore, northern NSW. It's a beautiful part of the world: lush and green with beaches, countryside and hippies. When I was 16, I couldn't decide if I wanted to be a radiographer or go into business. I had to choose my subjects for year 12 and time was running out. I approached the head of the x-ray unit at Lismore Base Hospital and asked if they would take me for two weeks' work experience. One of the radiologists was so enthusiastic about my interest in radiology, he took me under his wing.

I saw a broad range of procedures, including CT scans, x-rays of broken bones, ultrasounds and angiograms. My mentor exposed me to so many different situations, before I knew it I had a lead suit on as I witnessed blood fly here and there, met patients and watched as much as I could.

One day, I was due to observe a CT scan. As I walked through the waiting area, I saw a woman dabbing her red, watery eyes with a handkerchief. She looked sad and worried. I figured she was waiting for a family member. I walked into the CT unit and the radiologist showed me the patient's prostate cancer on the screen.

"What do you do now?" I asked.

"Did you see the lady out in the waiting room?" the radiologist asked. "She's this patient's wife. We have to go and speak with her."

In that moment, I felt so much sadness and pain for the

patient's family. I realised that I absorbed people's feelings a little too much, and was better suited to helping people in more positive situations. I decided to embark on a business degree instead of pursuing radiology.

Who would have known that years later, I would draw on this experience to help my clients today?

I have since had the privilege of working with young doctors and helping them achieve their dreams of becoming specialists in their fields. I am humbled by their extraordinary commitment to patient care and achieving their goals. They inspire me to strive towards my own goals, and demonstrate that we are capable of more than we think we are.

They also remind me that there are kind, caring and intelligent doctors out there who strive to make a difference for humanity.

This book is dedicated to doctors and their patients.

— **Jane Anderson**

CHAPTER 1

WHY DOES SELLING YOURSELF MATTER?

Congratulations! You have persevered through nearly a decade of intense study and rigorous training to become a qualified doctor. It takes an incredibly strong intellect and the utmost dedication to get to this point. You know what specialty training program you want to get in to and now it's time to prepare for your panel interview.

A strong intellect helps, of course, when it comes to your panel interview. The trouble is, nearly everyone else applying for the same medical specialty training program as you is equally as intelligent.

A panel interview is a whole different ball game to the years of study and training you have completed. Relying on your marks and achievements alone will not guarantee you success. To be in the coveted small percentage of doctors who get into their ideal specialty training program the first time around, you need to stand out from the crowd. You need to make a lasting impression.

You need to *sell yourself*.

What does it mean?

Selling yourself doesn't mean being cocky or arrogant. It

doesn't mean beating your chest and shouting, "Look at me! See how great I am?" Selling yourself means feeling confident. It's the ability to effectively communicate your skills and assets. It's about being in control during your interview.

Panel interviews can be scary if you're not prepared. The panellists usually show little emotion, which makes it difficult to know if what you're saying is hitting the mark. And when you're unsure, you can feel flustered. Your confidence nosedives. You stumble through your answers to the panellists' questions, and you may leave the interview feeling as though you'll have to try again next year, or even apply for another specialty.

You can avoid all this inner turmoil by understanding how to sell yourself!

Over the past 10 years, I have helped thousands of clients to position and market themselves to land their dream job. I have worked in human resources and on recruitment panels for government departments and some of Australia's fastest-growing organisations. A lot of my time has been spent coaching people on how to progress to senior roles.

I'm not a doctor and I don't profess to be one. However, I have worked with countless medical trainees and I know how to translate your skills into what the medical interview panel wants to hear. I will show you the techniques you need to know so you can connect with and impress the panel. With this book, you can gain the confidence to sell yourself and win a place on your specialty training program!

How 'interview ready' are you?

At this point in time, you probably don't know how to sell yourself well. You may be concerned about selling yourself too little or too much. In Australia, we have what's known as the "tall poppy syndrome", where it's undesirable to stand out. This syndrome is so entrenched in our culture, that the very idea of promoting yourself may make you feel uncomfortable. You don't want to appear boastful or brash during your interview, but you also don't want to miss out on your training program.

Take a look at the following model and see what level you are at. This will help you know what areas you need to improve on before you walk into your medical training interview. The model applies to most doctors I work with, who fall somewhere above (external) or below (internal) the line. There can be a marked difference between what they *do* (their activity) during their interview, and what they should be *doing* (focus).

CONFIDENCE IN MEDICAL INTERVIEWS				
		ACTIVITY	FOCUS	% CONFIDENCE
EXTERNAL	5	Agile	Practice	100
EXTERNAL	4	Structured	Evidence	50
EXTERNAL	3	Frustrated	Competencies	25
INTERNAL	2	Fearful	Panel	0
INTERNAL	1	Verbose	Brevity	-10

© Jane Anderson 2016

5

- **Level 1:** If you are at this lowest level, you are verbose. You talk too much and offer too much irrelevant information to the panel. You may feel under-prepared and your nerves are out of control. The amount of confidence you have at this level is generally in the negative and working against you.

- **Level 2:** You are fearful. You're unsure of what to say and are afraid of saying the wrong thing, so you don't say enough. The problem is that the panel does not have sufficient information about your skills, so it gives you a low score. You need to switch your focus from how you're feeling to what the panel wants to hear. Your confidence at this level is generally zero.

- **Level 3:** Most of my clients are at this level. They may have gone through the interview process more than once and feel frustrated that they're not getting anywhere. This is commonly caused by practising with and getting feedback from the wrong people: well-intentioned family or friends who don't understand the reality of the interview process. If you're at this level, you need to focus on your competencies (the areas of expertise the panel is looking for) to boost your confidence.

- **Level 4:** You know what the competencies are and you're able to anticipate the panel's questions. When you're at this level, you must focus on providing evidence to support your claims and demonstrate why you are the right person for the training program. Once you reach this level, your confidence is half-way to full potential.

- **Level 5:** At this top level, you have laid the foundation for a successful panel interview. You are clear about what the competencies are, can anticipate the questions you will be asked and know how to sell yourself. When you're at this level, you need to focus on practising your answers and self-selling techniques so your confidence can reach 100 per cent of what's possible.

As you can see, the difference between a person at level 1 and a person at level 5 is enormous. But don't lose heart: it is entirely possible for you to rise through the levels and learn how to successfully sell yourself to the interview panel. They key to this is *confidence*.

One of the common mistakes I see people make is that they start practising their answers to anticipated panel questions far too early. This is a level 5 activity, not a level 1, 2 or 3. If you haven't laid the foundation to prepare and move through the levels, you'll be practising the wrong answers and you won't get high marks during your interview. It's a bit like an iceberg: the practice questions are what you see on the surface, but there's a whole lot of work that needs to happen underneath before the questions can be answered with confidence.

CASE STUDY

In June 2014, I worked with a young female doctor called Melissa, whose ambition was to get on to the dermatology training program. She was incredibly bright, committed and passionate, yet she had been trying for five years to get on to her program. Why was it taking her so long to get an interview?

The problem was she had been receiving well-intentioned

but unhelpful feedback from her family. Although they were supportive and wanted to help Melissa with her interview preparations, her family had never been on a medical interview panel before. They had no understanding of the process or what the panellists thought at a conscious or subconscious level. They had never been involved in marking selection criteria or assessing capability. Their feedback was doing more harm than good, and Melissa's confidence plummeted.

After just four coaching sessions with me, Melissa managed to get an interview and was so successful, she got on to the dermatology training program. Naturally, she was thrilled! She had worked incredibly hard and had followed every direction I gave her. In her first session, she cried; not because she was sad, but because she was so relieved to find out where she had been going wrong and it all made perfect sense to her.

Melissa's story demonstrates that relying on the feedback of well-meaning family and friends can potentially hinder your chances of success. Although it's important to have the support of your loved ones, you need to get into the mind of a panellist and understand the specific interview skills required. This book will show you how.

Interpersonal skills vs interview skills

People often think strong interpersonal skills are what's needed for a successful interview. I have worked with doctors who have had incredibly strong interpersonal skills. But in my experience, the doctors who *do not* have good interpersonal skills are the ones who are able to sell themselves well during an interview. This is because they are not focused on trying to read the faces of the panellists, which would otherwise distract them from answering questions confidently.

The people I see struggle with panel interviews are the ones who are emotionally intelligent, kind and compassionate doctors. They are exceptionally good at what they do because of their interpersonal skills. They are often incredibly humble: an admirable quality, but one that causes them to struggle during interviews. It is difficult for them to switch from the role of a caring and understanding doctor to confident salesperson.

Blitzing an interview is not about having superior social skills: it's about having the conviction that you do stand out from the crowd. It's the ability to demonstrate this to the panel.

It's about *confidence*.

CHAPTER 2
HOW TO GET CONFIDENCE

"Always be yourself and have faith in yourself.
Do not go out and look for a successful personality and try to duplicate it."
— Bruce Lee

Confidence is vital to a successful medical interview. It guides the way you present and sell yourself, which in turn impacts the way the panel perceives you and your abilities. In other words, confidence (or a lack of it) can make or break your interview. But how do you become confident? Some people seem to be naturally confident, but for others it is hard work, no matter how skilled or intelligent they are.

They key to building your confidence is *being prepared*.

Learn to read the game

Imagine you are about to play a tennis match against Roger Federer, one of the greatest tennis players of all time. Would you simply walk on to the court, cross your fingers and hope for the best? Of course not! You would be annihilated. To stand any sort of chance, you would need to do your research and understand Federer's style of game.

It is the same with your medical interview. You need to read the panel's game. You need to be mentally agile enough to anticipate the panel's questions and hit back with the right answers. Otherwise, it will be game over.

You can push the odds in your favour

The odds of you getting on to your desired specialty training program are low. There are many different medical training programs and the interview can count for a different percentage of your application, depending on the program.

The good news is, 80 per cent of the young doctors I have coached have been selected for their chosen program in their first attempt after being coached by me. How did this happen? They learnt to read the game and built their confidence by focusing on the following three areas:

1. Competencies
2. Questions
3. Practice

These three areas are explained by the following **Interview Readiness Model**.

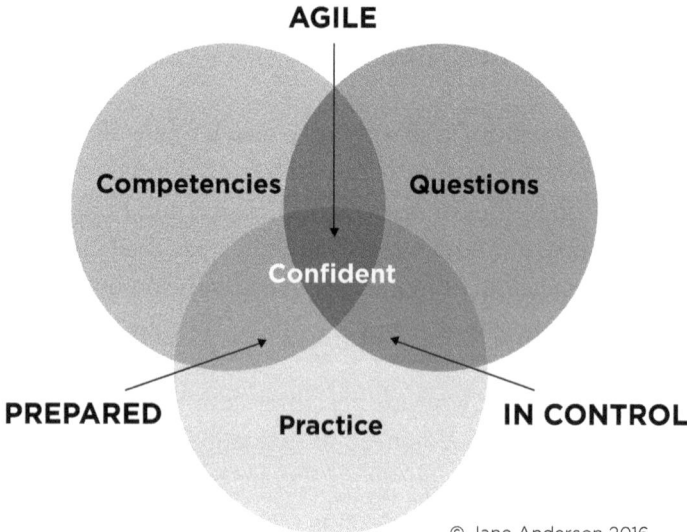

© Jane Anderson 2016

1. **Competencies:** Each speciality has a set of competencies (areas of expertise) the panel is looking for. Most are underpinned by the competencies of the Royal Australian College of Surgeons (RACS), but there will be some variation. If the competencies for your specialty are not clear, I recommend you familiarise yourself with the RACS competencies. Knowing the competencies will make you mentally agile in your interview. You will know what skills you need to sell, you will understand the mindset of the panel and you can anticipate the questions you will be asked.

- *At the intersection of Competencies and Questions:* You will feel *agile* instead of feeling as though you are being pushed around by the panel. The more you can move quickly and ahead of the panel, the more your confidence increases.

2. **Questions:** Not knowing what the panel will ask creates a great amount of stress. Being interview ready means anticipating the questions you will be asked, and rehearsing your responses to them. Getting feedback from a coach or mentor who understands the process well will help you craft compelling answers. You need to be able to answer a range of questions, from standard questions such as, "Tell us about yourself," to behavioural and ethics-based questions (we will look at these kinds of questions in Chapter 6).

- *At the intersection of Questions and Practice:* You will be *in control* instead of a sitting duck. When you feel in control, your confidence soars. You know where you're taking the panel with your answers, instead of the panel being in control of you.

3. **Practice:** Your schedule leading up to the interview is crucial. As a doctor, you have a busy roster and time is of the essence. Preparing for days on end is not going to work. In the months leading to your interview, you need to schedule in the appropriate amount of time to get into the right head space so you can prepare and practise your answers effectively. Practising also helps manage your stress levels, as you will feel confident that you can answer any question the panel throws at you. Practice helps you feel in control during your interview.

- *At the intersection of Practice and Competencies:* You will be *prepared* instead of nervous. Preparation is key to your confidence and it will help you stand out against the other candidates.

- *Centre: Confidence.* Ultimately, this is what you need to be able to walk into your interview and sell yourself. Without it, you won't stand out from the crowd and you won't impress the panel.

How do I get started?

The first step towards becoming interview ready is to have a full comprehension of the interview process and the nature of the panel. Chapter 3 will explain what you can expect during your panel interview.

CHAPTER 3

PANELS AND INTERVIEWS

Specialty training programs are highly competitive. Only a small number of candidates are accepted into their desired program the first time around. It is the interviewing panel's role to select only the very best doctors for a specialty training program. This makes your role as candidate a challenging one.

Who is on a panel?

A panel consists of a number of experts who have been recruited based on their high level of knowledge. This could range from three panellists to 10 or more. These professionals all bring their unique insights to the judging panel as they search for different skills and qualities in each candidate. For example, a panel may include a professor who understands the technical skills required for a training program. It may also include a psychologist who can detect the personality traits suited to a specialty. Having a range of experts helps the panel gain a well-rounded understanding of each candidate.

How does it work?

A panel interview can be intimidating. If you go in not knowing what to expect, it can feel as though you are facing a firing squad: you sit before a group of experts who show little emotion as they fire question after question. All you want to do is duck for cover.

The reason for this cold, almost aggressive situation is that the panel usually does not want to build a rapport with you. In fact, it's to the panel's advantage that you don't feel comfortable so it can assess how you react under pressure. Australian medical interviews contrast starkly with the process in America, where candidates are often walked around the hospital and even invited to dinner!

Multiple mini interviews

Many specialties in Australia conduct a multiple mini interview (MMI), rather than a standard panel interview. The MMI consists of different stations – usually eight – with a different interviewer and scenario at each. You have a strict time limit in which to answer questions about a scenario, before you must move to the next station. The MMI can take up to two hours to complete.

Typically, the scenarios and questions posed in the MMI relate to ethical dilemmas. These are designed to test your ability to deal with your own emotions and the emotions of others in stressful situations.

The importance of cut-through

In his book *Brief*, communications expert Joe McCormack says the average person can absorb 650 words per minute, but can only speak 150 words per minute. This is why it is so important to have cut-through – or impact – when speaking to the interviewing panel. Panellists are human, after all, and sometimes they do not pay 100% attention to everything you say. You need to ensure sure your words count by making them relevant, concise and engaging.

You also can't assume all the panellists have read your resume and application. If you've worked at a certain hospital or undertaken certain training, let them know during your interview – and be specific with the details. You know you have the skills and fortitude for your desired training program. Make the panel's job easier by spelling it out for them!

Unintentional bias

Panellists must be shrewd with the way they score. They need to be able to justify their scores with clear evidence of why or why not a candidate is suitable for a training program, and prevent unintentional bias from impacting their judgement.

I have trained panels on how to recruit and have been on a number of interviewing panels myself, and I have seen unintentional bias at play – to the detriment of the panel and the candidate. On one particular panel, two panellists scored the candidate highly, while the third panellist gave a very low score. The two panellists who gave a high score already knew the candidate, having seen them perform in a similar role. They naturally gave a high score, even though the candidate had failed to effectively articulate their skills and suitability for the role during the interview. The third panellist had no bias, was not impressed by the candidate and gave a low score. The candidate may have relied too much on the favour of the first two panellists without trying to sell to the third.

While procedures are in place to prevent unintentional bias during medical training interviews, it can happen. It's important that you can sell yourself with clear-cut evidence of why you are suitable for your chosen training program, even if you happen to know somebody on the interviewing panel.

How a panel scores you

Panellists have a marking guide that helps them score a candidate against certain criteria. The guide allows them to objectively determine whether a candidate has the required skills and meets the competencies of the specialty training program. It also helps the panellists maintain their focus on what you are saying, as they don't have to write copious notes.

The following is an example of a typical marking guide.

Question: Give an example of when you have used your interpersonal skills to give bad news to a patient.

RESPONSES	SCORE
Context 1. Medical situation described.	
Goal/Tasks 2. Identifies what needs to be done.	
Actions taken 3. Approached in a calm and friendly manner, smiled, introduced themselves and job.	
4. Sat beside them rather than across the table, offered water.	
5. Explained why they were there.	

6. Displayed empathy and understanding to the patient by saying things such as, "I understand, this must be challenging," etc.	
7. Gave time and space for the patient to react.	
8. Acknowledged patient's feelings and kept calm.	
9. Liaised with nursing staff.	
10. Gave details for any further questions.	
11. Followed up with: • Patient • Colleagues • Mentor or supervisor for feedback	
12. Made any changes or improvement to processes in the hospital as a result.	
13. Achieved positive outcomes for: • Patient • Hospital	
14. If not, learnt from the situation and has made changes in future.	
15. Used as a learning opportunity for others (i.e. integrated into teaching or mentoring others).	
TOTAL SCORE:	

As the marking guide shows, you will receive a score for the different areas you address in your answer. These individual scores add up to a total score for that question.

- If you fail to address any criterion, you will get a 0.
- If you address the context, you may get a mark.
- If you address the context and goal/tasks, you might get 2 marks.
- If you address the context, goal/tasks and actions taken, you will likely receive 3½ or 4 marks.
- If you address all the criteria, including the results, you will likely receive all 5 marks.

Here is an example of an answer that would possibly gain full marks:

Question: Why did you apply for the cosmetic surgery training program?

I applied for this program for cosmetic surgery because I've had various years of experience in the surgical field. I've been exposed to many different kinds of operations and understand the intricacy of an operation as a whole, including preparation, planning and looking after the patient post-surgery.

I have worked in different kinds of health-care constructs, in the public and private systems, the rural system and the metropolitan system. I've been involved in research and trained registrars and students. I've also been involved with feedback with the consultants, mobility, frozen shoulders and mortality meetings, and I understand how we can improve our system.

I have presented at various conferences, including Las Vegas and Paris. That experience has helped me with the college training. I also think that my technical skill has improved over the years and I've had various colleagues call me when they have had difficulty doing an operation. I assist them and we're able to complete the operation together. Sometimes, I simply provide a different perspective, but behind this is my breadth of experience and understanding.

I'm a great communicator and I'm often told by my peers and patients that I'm really approachable. I am able to develop a positive rapport with patients, and I find I can get a lot more information from them than most other doctors or surgeons can. In fact, I have had colleagues consult me when they've had a difficult patient, asking me for advice on how to get their patient to give them the information they need.

I'm also adaptable and here to learn new operations and learn new skills. Cosmetics is new to me and there are lots of things I'd like to learn, so I am committed to my professional development.

The other thing I'm highly skilled at is organising journal clubs. I've been involved with 25 journal clubs over the past few years. We have run five to 10 a year and I've organised them all – getting the articles, emailing the consultants and getting feedback. My ability to do this means we can always progress our research and have an ever-developing cosmetic surgical college. A lot of work is involved but it's rewarding because, professionally, we all get to know each other. We know what our deficiencies are and how we can improve.

So, I've applied for this training program because of my skill set, which I think would be highly beneficial to you. I have the experience, and I know that with your guidance, I can excel and contribute to the profession as a cosmetic surgeon.

The marking guide is a vital tool for the panel – and it's gold for you. It gives you a valuable insight into the mind of a panellist: what they're looking for in a candidate and what they want to hear from you. Use the marking guide as you formulate your answers in the lead-up to your interview. It will keep what you say concise and on track. The panellists will be engaged by what you say and you'll leave a lasting impression.

CHAPTER 4

COMPETENCIES

To have any sort of chance of getting into your medical training program, you must demonstrate to the interviewing panel that you have the competencies required of your desired specialty.

What is a competency?

A competency is an ability, skill or characteristic that can be objectively measured against a pre-determined standard. Examples include patient care, clinical expertise and analytical skills. Essentially, they are selection criteria for a training program. Competencies enable the panel to assess candidates objectively, and signal to the panel whether or not you are likely to succeed as a specialist trainee.

Know your competencies

The Royal Australian College of Surgeons (RACS) stipulates nine competencies to ensure specialist surgeons "facilitate safe, comprehensive surgical care of the highest standard". They are:

- Collaboration and teamwork
- Communication
- Health advocacy
- Judgement – clinical decision making
- Management and leadership
- Medical expertise
- Professionalism and ethics

- Scholarship and teaching
- Technical expertise

RACS provides a training standards framework for these nine competencies, which is used by specialty and training boards when determining their own competency requirements. You can find out more about the RACS competencies here: http://www.surgeons.org/becoming-a-surgeon/surgical-education-training/competencies/

While it's important for you to know the nine RACS competencies, different specialties stipulate different competencies. Few of the young doctors I have worked with had even *read* their competencies before I started coaching them. It's to your significant advantage that you have a thorough understanding of the competencies so you can sell yourself to the panel with confidence.

To find out about your specialty's competencies, you must visit the website of that speciality and look for the competencies. They will usually be listed in the area associated with the requirements to get onto the training programs.

Examples of specialties and their competencies

Dermatology

- Being proactive
- Showing altruistic patient focus
- Demonstrating interpersonal understanding and empathy to all work colleagues, supervisors and patients
- Using intuitive/holistic thinking
- Following things through to completion

For more information: https://www.dermcoll.edu.au/ become-dermatologist-2/australian-medical-graduates/ selection-process/interviewing/

Obstetrics and gynaecology (RANZCOG)

- Academic ability
- Clinical expertise
- Professional qualities

For more information: http://www.ranzcog.edu.au/how-do-i-apply68/selection-process.html (see the application form scoring guidelines)

Oral and maxillofacial surgery

- Professional skills and communication
- Ethics
- Academic skills
- Patient care
- Preparation for OMS training

For more information: https://www.racds.org/documents/ Handbooks/OMS%20Handbook.pdf

Australian General Practice Training Program

- Communication and interpersonal skills
- Clinical reasoning
- Analytical/problem-solving skills
- Organisational/management skills
- Sense of vocation/motivation
- Personal attributes
- Professional/ethical attributes

For more information: http://www.gpet.com.au/Junior-
doctors/Australian-General-Practice-Training--AGPT-
-program/New-Applicants/Application-and-selection-
process/Stage-Two---National-Assessment

Knowing your competencies ensures you won't fly blind
during your interview. However, knowing what skills and
attributes the panel is looking for in a candidate is not enough.
You must be able to concisely and effectively *demonstrate* your
competencies during your interview.

Sell your competencies

From the panel's perspective, interviewing candidates is a bit
like listening to the radio. If a radio station goes out of range,
all you hear is static. It's annoying and you're likely to switch
off. Similarly, in a panel interview, if the candidate goes off
topic, says too much and offers the panel too much irrelevant
information (static), the panel struggles to get to the heart
of what they're trying to say. The panellists will tire of sifting
through the verbal clutter and switch off, hoping that the next
candidate is more eloquent. The candidate who is "in tune" by
clearly demonstrating their competencies is the one who gets
top marks.

Identify the tasks and activities you have performed that
can prove to the panel you have achieved the competencies
required. Here are some RACS competencies and examples of
associated activities you could share with the panel:

Communication

• Communicating across a range of specialists and staff in

the hospital, including in indigenous communities and overseas

- Liaising with a variety of patients and their families and how this enabled you to establish positive relationships
- Working in another country
- Delivering bad news
- Challenging a supervisor
- Presenting at conferences and events
- Showing empathy

Management and leadership

- Involvement in committees and meetings
- Making changes to processes or continuous improvement
- Giving feedback and training
- Managing under-performing staff
- Managing resources and budgets

Clinical decision making

- Explain how you have arrived at a well-reasoned diagnosis of a patient. Give examples of when you have:
  - o Recognised symptoms in the area of expertise
  - o Managed critically ill patients
  - o Performed accurate assessments of patients
  - o Evaluated alternatives of treatment and outcomes for patients
  - o Managed complex cases

Scholarship and teaching

- Attending conferences and training programs
- Undertaking further mentoring and supervision
- Facilitating learning in communities

- Undertaking research
- Training others, tutoring or lecturing
- Research translation

Professionalism and ethics

- Identifying ethical issues
- Maintaining appropriate relationships with patients
- Acknowledging your own limitations
- Peer reviews
- Identifying conflicts of interest

Take the time to thoroughly investigate your specialty's competencies and concisely pinpoint how you have achieved them. It will keep the panellists engaged during your interview and will encourage them to give you top marks.

CHAPTER 5

QUESTIONS AND ANSWERS

Selling yourself during your interview means confidently answering any question the panel throws at you. There are four key elements to forming a compelling answer. They are:

1. Content
2. Supporting your claims
3. Structure
4. Timing

Content

Whatever the question is, your answer needs to address the competencies of your specialty. Remember, you need to be in tune with what the panel wants to hear so you get top marks.

Keep your answers focused on the tasks relevant to the competencies. Don't assume the panel has read your resume – spell out your achievements, experience and training. Tell the panel about the conditions you've seen and operated on, the research you've undertaken and clinical trials you've conducted. You also need to highlight your skills, such as interpersonal and communication skills, teaching skills and team skills.

Different specialties have different buzz words and terms. For example, "manual dexterity" is a buzz term in surgery. Including buzz words in your answers emphasises your experience and understanding of the specialty.

Support your claims

Simply telling the panel that you have completed a task doesn't mean you have done it well. You need to build the panel's trust in you by supporting your claims with evidence showing you have been effective at your tasks.

For example, to demonstrate the RACS competency of Scholar and Teacher, and to prove your effectiveness, you could detail a presentation you have made and cite the positive feedback you received from your supervisor.

Other examples of supporting evidence include:

- Performance reviews.
- Peers consulting you for advice on a particular topic, or instances where they've sought guidance from you if they've had a difficult patient.
- The number of presentations you have made on a particular topic.
- The amount of time you have spent in a unit (eg. two years instead of a standard six-month rotation).

Structure

Structure is key to a concise, easily understood answer. By offering a rambling response, or only partly answering a question, you risk losing all-important marks.

Structuring your content requires care and attention. It's similar to making a cake. You need to make sure all the ingredients are there and follow the method in the right order before the cake can come out of the oven perfect and ready for icing. Many of my clients initially ignore the hard work and just go straight for the icing!

To make your structure work, you need to do the following three things:

1. Link to the competencies.
2. Explain how you have achieved the competencies by citing the tasks you have undertaken.
3. Demonstrate how effective you have been at these tasks.

It's important your answers do all of these three things, and in the correct order. For example, I once had a client called Candice, who was applying for dermatology. She was giving low-scoring answers during her interview preparations. She would start well by addressing a particular competency and discussing the associated tasks she had undertaken, but she would let herself down by failing to demonstrate how effective she had been.

Her answers sounded like the following:

"I have a high level of interpersonal and communication skills. I have spoken at five conferences and delivered poster presentations and research.

"I also lecture part time at UQ to over 100 students."

On a scale of one to five, her answers were generally a score of 1½ to 2 out of 5.

If Candice had structured her answers with the goal of achieving as many marks as possible, her content would have sounded more like the following:

ANSWER STRUCTURE		
COMPETENCY	**HOW YOU DEMONSTRATED**	**EFFECTIVENESS**
I applied because I have a high level of interpersonal and communication skills.	I have undertaken rural placements, as well as urban, and have learnt to deal with a broad range of patients. I have spoken at five conferences and delivered poster presentations and research. I also lecture part time at UQ to over 100 students on X specialty.	My team often consults me for advice on how to deal with difficult patients and their families. On my last rotation, my consultant gave me feedback in my review that it was one of my strengths.

© Jane Anderson 2016

So, when framing your responses, ensure you have covered all aspects of the question, including the competency you're addressing, how you demonstrated it and how you know you've been effective. You will have far more impact with your answers and gain more marks from the panel.

Timing

Be succinct with your answers. Every word you choose must give you the highest-possible return on investment. This ensures you cut out the static so you don't bore the panel with a long-winded answer.

Aim to answer standard questions (eg. "Tell us about yourself") in two minutes. Behavioural questions (eg. "What are your weaknesses?") require a slightly longer response of three to four minutes.

At first, it can be difficult to get this timing right, as an interview is the complete opposite of a normal conversation. Typically, people speak in 30-second blocks for a balanced conversation: 30 seconds for me, then 30 seconds for you, and so on. In an interview, the conversation is unbalanced: the interviewer speaks for five seconds, then you have to speak for minutes at a time. It goes against all the interpersonal and social skills you have learnt, so it's easy to get nervous and say too much or too little.

One way of getting your timing right is to write your answers, then time yourself as you recite them aloud. Reduce any redundant content or add relevant content as necessary.

THE RULE OF THREE

Another way to keep your answers succinct is by using "the rule of three". The rule of three is based on the premise that three is the most powerful and persuasive number in communication. It is easier to remember three chunks of information than, say, eight or 12.

Entrepreneur Steve Jobs used the rule of three in almost every presentation he made. In 2007, he said Apple would be releasing *three* revolutionary products – a new iPod, a new phone and a new internet communications device. In 2010, he launched the first iPad, which would come in *three* models. In 2011, he launched the iPad 2, which was *"thinner, lighter* and *faster"*.

The rule of three can be seen everywhere: in titles (eg. *The Three Musketeers, Three Blind Mice*), catchphrases and slogans (eg. "Slip, Slop, Slap", "Stop, Look, Listen", "Work, Rest, Play"), and book and performance structure (eg. beginning, middle and end; three-act plays). It's also evident in the affirmation made by witnesses in court ("... the truth, the whole truth, and nothing but the truth").

The rule of three will help you make a real impact during your interview. Think of it as hammering a nail: the first hit makes a nice dent, the second drives the nail in further, and the third puts the nail perfectly in place. Anything more or less doesn't quite have the same impact.

The rule of three will also help you remember the content and structure of your answers, so you're less likely to stumble during your interview.

Now that you know the elements of formulating a compelling answer, it's time to focus on the kinds of questions you'll be answering during your interview. The panel's marking guide and the competencies of your specialty give you a good indication, but you still can't know exactly what you'll be asked.

What you *can* do is become mentally agile enough to take on the curliest of questions. How can you achieve this? You need to prepare for the Magic Five Questions.

The Magic Five Questions

The Magic Five Questions will arm you with answers for almost any question. The panel might not ask you these specific questions, but your answers to them will provide you with a blueprint to call upon during your interview.

In his book *The Power of Habit*, Charles Duhigg explains how the military's requirement for beds to be made first thing in the morning is a "keystone habit". The significance of making the beds is not about keeping quarters tidy – it's about discipline. Starting the day with an act of order and organisation – a keystone habit – reinforces discipline and sets the tone for the rest of the day.

The Magic Five Questions provide you with a keystone habit. They require discipline and focus. Preparing your answers and scheduling the time to practice them puts you into the mindset of a confident self-seller. Learning to sell yourself with these five questions will make you mentally agile enough to answer all kinds of questions.

In the following section, I will explain each of the Magic Five Questions and demonstrate how they should and should not be answered. I will also provide examples of answers scored on a scale of one to five.

1. Tell us about yourself.

This seemingly innocuous question has two purposes: it is an ice breaker to get you talking, and it's a way for you to demonstrate your experience. It's not the time for you to talk about your love of sport or your family; it's a vehicle for you to encapsulate your skills and capabilities relating to the competencies.

Keep in mind that people usually make an unconscious judgement about someone within the first 10 seconds of meeting them. As Margaret Thatcher once said, "Generally, I make a decision about one in the first 10 seconds, and I usually find I'm right."

The panellists may pigeonhole you without even realising it, so you need to work hard with this first question to have maximum impact. If your answer is verbose and unfocused, you face an uphill battle for the rest of the interview. If you keep your answer succinct and on track, you will feel confident and the panel will be engaged by what you say.

Your answer to this question should be about two minutes. This may seem like a short amount of time, but I find that 99% of my clients initially struggle to speak about themselves for this long for fear of boring the panel or saying the wrong thing. You can avoid this by focusing on your competencies.

For example, if you're applying for dermatology, be specific about the conditions you've had experience with, such as skin cancers and psoriasis. If you're applying for geriatrics, you may have encountered patients with dementia and Parkinson's disease.

Examples of scores:

- **2/5:** You mention at a broad level what you have done:

  "I've worked with people who have presented a range of skin conditions."

- **3.5/5:** You mention at a specific level some of your experience:

  "I've spent the past six years working with patients who have presented a range of skin conditions, including skin cancers and psoriasis."

- **4.5-5/5:** You mention at a specific level all relevant work experience, including clinics you've worked in, procedures and clinical trials conducted, presentations made, conferences attended and volunteer work undertaken:

  "I've spent the past six years – including four years at X Medical Centre and two years at Y Medical Centre – diagnosing patients who have presented a range of skin conditions, including skin cancers, psoriasis and seborrhoeic keratosis. I have conducted a range of tests – including biopsies, scrapings and diascopies – to successfully diagnose skin disorders."

2. Why did you apply for the program?

It's easy to think that this question indicates the panel cares about you, or is interested to know your personal mission. This is incorrect. This is a *selling yourself* question.

A wrong answer is this:

"Well, I've always been really interested in this specialty. I'm passionate and hard working and this is the program for me."

These things may be true, but it's what the majority of candidates say. This kind of answer fails to address any of the competencies. It doesn't demonstrate that you are a perfect fit for the program, and it doesn't make you stand out from the crowd. You need to flip your focus from what's in it for you to what's in it for the panel. Your answer needs to say: "This is the problem you've got and this is what I have to solve it."

For example:

"I applied for this program because you said you wanted someone who has good interpersonal skills and can work as part of a team."

Demonstrate these skills by explaining the tasks you've undertaken, and support your claims with evidence showing you've been effective.

You should answer this question in two minutes. Remember to use "the rule of three" to keep your answer concise.

Examples of scores:

- **1.5-2/5:** You mention what's in it for you:

  "I'm passionate about this field. After my rotation at X hospital, I discovered I had a strong interest. I'm hard working and I think I have what it takes."

- **3.5/5:** You mention at a specific level the competencies and demonstrate the skills the panel is looking for:

   "I applied for this program as I have strong interpersonal skills and am committed to research. For the past year, I've been working with a team of seven doctors conducting a case-control study to assess the relationship between cervical cancer and the use of oral contraceptives."

- **4.5-5/5:** You mention at a specific level the competencies and demonstrate the skills the panel is looking for. You also provide supporting evidence demonstrating that you were effective:

   "I applied for this program as I have strong interpersonal skills and am committed to research. For two years, I worked with a team of seven doctors conducting a case-control study to assess the relationship between cervical cancer and the use of oral contraceptives. The study was so successful that our paper is due to be published next year."

3. What are your strengths?

Your answer to this question needs to show the panel that your personal skills and traits make you a perfect fit for the training program. Like the second question, it's about being able to sell yourself with confidence.

When discussing your strengths, you need to be very clear about what competencies and tasks they relate to. Simply saying, "I'm hard working, inquisitive and have a strong eye for detail," is not enough. You need to show how these qualities are relevant to the specialty. For example, to demonstrate your diligence, you could explain how you came to a successful diagnosis of a patient whose case was particularly difficult and time consuming.

You should answer this question in about two minutes.

Examples of scores:

- **1.5-2/5:** You mention a series of skills that *are not* in the selection criteria:

  "I'm passionate and have a good eye for detail. I'm hard working and will do what it takes to get a result."

- **3.5/5:** You mention skills that *are* specified in the selection criteria and give evidence to demonstrate them:

  "My strengths lie in my commitment to health advocacy and leadership skills. I have managed a team of three to develop a public awareness campaign in the Alice Springs community that encourages indigenous people to get their yearly flu shots."

- **4.5/5:** You mention at a specific level three skills in the selection criteria and explain tasks undertaken to demonstrate them. You provide supporting evidence that shows you have been effective at these tasks, such as feedback from a supervisor or awards received:

  "My strengths lie in my commitment to health advocacy, my leadership qualities and my

communication skills. I have managed a team of three to develop a public awareness campaign in the Alice Springs community that encourages indigenous people to get their yearly flu shots. Since the beginning of the campaign 18 months ago, the number of indigenous people getting their yearly flu shots has risen by 20%."

4. What are your weaknesses?

It may seem as though this question is designed to throw you off track, but its aim is to assess two things: your level of self-awareness and your level of self-management.

The last thing a supervisor wants is to have to manage you constantly. Your answer to this question lets the panel know if you are aware of your flaws, and whether you have the capacity to self-correct them.

Many of my clients believe this question is an opportunity for them to present their weaknesses as strengths. In my opinion, this is a misapprehension. It is impossible to manipulate a weakness into a strength, but the way you answer this question can bring the direction of the interview back to your favour.

To demonstrate, on the following page is a model called **Above and Below the Line**.

Above and Below the Line

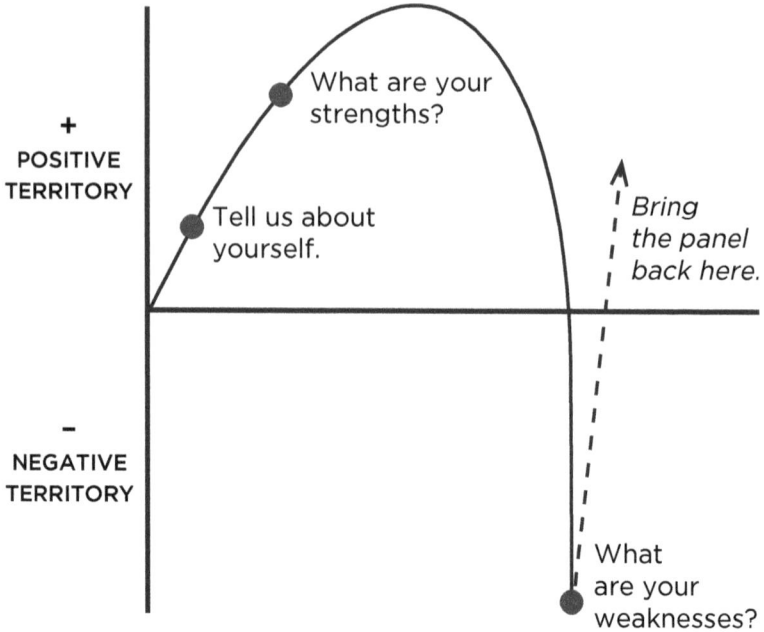

What are your strengths?

+
POSITIVE
TERRITORY

Tell us about yourself.

Bring the panel back here.

−
NEGATIVE
TERRITORY

What are your weaknesses?

© Jane Anderson 2016

The majority of your interview will be "above the line". The panel will ask you positive questions, such as: "Tell us about yourself", "What are your strengths?" and "Why have you applied for the program?" At some point, however, the panel will bring you into negative territory – "below the line". "What are your weaknesses?" is a below-the-line question. It's your job to bring the interview back into a positive space – not by denying the fact you have weaknesses, but by showing you take personal responsibility for them.

You won't get above the line with negative wording such as: "My weakness is …," "My problem is …," or "My issue is …"

This underlines what you *don't* want to be known for. But you also can't say: "Weaknesses? I don't have any!" This shows you have no self-awareness, which is a dangerous thing for a doctor (and yes, one of my clients has said this!).

This question isn't about the panel wanting to know that you're perfect. It's about giving you the opportunity to show you're aware you have areas you need to improve on, and that you're doing something about it.

Examples of scores:

- **1.5-2/5:** You list a series of skills that are in the selection criteria:

  "I'm very aware of my weaknesses and the impact they can have on patient care. I feel that one of my weaknesses is that I can be a perfectionist and lose time trying to achieve solutions for patients.

  "Another one of my weaknesses is that I can spend too long with patients at times, which can have an impact on resources. This is something I have been working on."

- **3.5/5:** You mention skills that *are not* specified in the selection criteria and give evidence to demonstrate them:

  "I'm very aware of my weaknesses and the impact they can have on patient care. I feel that one of my weaknesses is that I can be a perfectionist and lose time trying to achieve solutions for patients. I have been working on this and I'm starting to see some results."

- **4.5-5/5:** You mention a skill (not more than one) that you've been trying to improve, the strategy you have implemented and how you know it's working:

  "Something I've been working on is my efficiency. I can sometimes lose too much time working with patients. I'm trying to become more effective and efficient at managing them so that I can reduce wait times. Some of the strategies I've implemented include planning my day well and if a patient has more than one condition, I'll ask them to come back for another appointment. I set clear expectations and what I'm noticing is that I'm not as stressed, I'm not behind, I'm not frustrating my staff and colleagues, and I'm not frustrating my patients. I've got a good rapport with them because they know I am pretty much on time."

This answer identifies an area you need to improve on, but quickly reassures the panel that it's not a permanent problem as you're taking action to correct it. You are highlighting your self-awareness and ability to self-manage, demonstrating that you're a good fit for the training program.

5. Why should we put you on the program?

This "selling yourself" question is similar to question number two ("Why did you apply for the program?"). The reason I am including this question in the Magic Five is not only to further enhance your self-selling training, but because it is highly likely that you will be asked two questions that are almost identical during your panel interview.

You need to focus your answer on the competencies of your

specialty to reinforce your suitability for the program. This is the time for you to really spell it out for the panel that you meet the criteria. Reiterate what you've done to achieve the competencies and give clear evidence of your effectiveness.

For example:

> *"I think I should be put on the program because I meet the criteria you're looking for. Based on what you've said, you need someone with a commitment to research and strong leadership skills. I have effectively managed my own team of researchers to conduct a clinical study, which was so successful that our paper has been published in a well-respected journal."*

Try to spend two to three minutes answering this question, addressing three to four competencies.

Here's an example of a great answer:

> *"I think you should put me on the program based on the skills you've said you're looking for. I have eight years of experience and have done thousands of operations. I have been exposed to various specialties in orthopaedics, neurosurgery, cardiovascular and general surgery, and I've worked in different hospital systems, public and private, in Australia and overseas. I've also worked in rural settings in other states, including Tasmania and the Northern Territory.*
>
> *"I've done a lot of research and have authored three papers. I've also been involved in five other*

papers that have been published. I realise how interesting research can be and the difference it makes in the field.

"I am committed to my own learning and have attended conferences both in Australia and internationally. They have increased my knowledge and confidence, as well as my networks with other medical experts.

"I've also been involved in the delivery of training and education, including six months of anatomy demonstration before hundreds of medical students.

"I think I can hit the ground running with this training program."

There is a lot to remember when formulating your answers to the Magic Five Questions. They require time, patience and focus, but the effort you put in will pay dividends during your panel interview. Write your answers, read them aloud and time them. Once you have refined them, it's time to move on to the practice phase.

During your interview, you will also be asked more specific questions relating to real and hypothetical situations that will help the panel predict your future behaviour, assess your ethics and determine your psychological make-up. We will explore these questions in Chapter 6.

CHAPTER 6

BEHAVIOURAL QUESTIONS

To make a thorough and accurate assessment of your suitability for a specialty training program, the panel not only needs to see that you have completed the required tasks and have the right skills – it needs to predict how you will act in certain situations.

The panel makes predictions about your future behaviour and judgements through the use of:

- Behavioural questions
- Ethical questions
- Psychometric profiling

Behavioural questions

Behavioural-based questions are designed to predict your future behaviour based on previous behaviour. The panel will ask you to describe a situation you have encountered and explain how you dealt with it.

You should aim to answer these questions in three to four minutes. To ensure your answer is well structured and concise, I recommend you use the STAR technique:

- **Situation:** Describe the situation and context.
- **Task:** Describe the goal – what you identified as needing to be done. You will ideally explain this in one sentence.

- **Action:** Describe what action you took and give specific details. This should comprise about 80% of your answer.
- **Result:** Describe the outcome.

Here is an example of answering a behavioural question using the STAR technique:

Tell us about a time when you made an improvement in a hospital setting.

Situation: During my role as the junior doctor representative of the medical steering committee at X Hospital, I identified that improvements could be made in the resident handover process between ward call shifts. One of the major issues facing junior doctors was an unstructured and ineffective handover process.

I knew this was a significant issue as I had experienced many ward call shifts and realised that handover was a critical period to ensure continuity of patient care. It is a time when mistakes are easily made, particularly when you're disrupted by nurses paging a ward call. I had personally experienced suboptimal handovers where incorrect patient details and locations were given to me.

I raised this issue with the medical steering committee and asked members for their thoughts. This was a challenge at first, as most of them – especially the medical administration officers – had never experienced a ward call.

Task: My goal was to create a better-quality handover

process that ensured continuity of patient care and reduced negative impacts on patients.

Action: I proposed a 30-minute protected ward call handover time, where nurses could only page calls in emergency situations. I also designed a ward call job-list template, which included the patient's name, ward and bed number, a brief job description and the number for the requesting nurse.

Although the committee supported the job-list template, initially some members did not understand why I had proposed a 30-minute handover. They thought a handover should take just a few minutes. I empathised with them by saying I realised it may seem like a lengthy amount of time, but 30 minutes was necessary to ensure a thorough handover and minimise the chance of error. To give the medical administration officers a better understanding, I organised for a committee member to observe one of my colleagues handing over a ward call shift using the new template.

I discussed with the committee the logistics of a protected 30-minute window for handover, and collectively we decided that for it to be effective, the template must be available to all staff via the Princess Alexandra Hospital website. By ensuring all members of the committee had a good understanding of the process, a consensus was reached and the initiative was implemented. We designed posters informing nurses and allied health professionals about the protected window, and displayed these in nursing stations in all the wards.

Result: The 30-minute protected window has since been implemented hospital-wide for all resident handovers. The medical steering committee chairperson thanked me for raising the issue. I emailed the chairperson five months later to check if any issues had arisen, but was informed that everything had gone smoothly.

Colleagues have also informed me that the longer window has reduced the number of mistakes made during handover, and has improved the structure of the handover process in general.

The following examples demonstrate the differences between a mediocre answer and an exceptional answer to a behavioural-based question that will get you top marks:

Tell us about a time when you showed empathy and understanding.

Typical answer:

Situation: I was working in a small hospital in western New South Wales in a unit for patients waiting to be placed in nursing homes or palliative care. An elderly man who had recently been diagnosed with a metastasis to the liver was admitted to our unit while he awaited placement in a nursing home. During his stay, he began rapidly declining and was dying. After a week, the nurse unit manager approached me to say she had phoned a palliative care unit and had found a bed for the elderly man. She said she wanted him transferred as it was costing our unit too much money to have him in a single-stay bed for longer than a week. The patient's son was very, very upset – he was worried the patient would die on the way to the palliative care unit, without dignity and in an unfamiliar environment. I agreed with him.

Task: My goal was to help manage the situation and maintain the patient's dignity.

Action: I requested a meeting with the nurse unit manager and the patient's son, and we sat down to discuss the situation. I explained the patient's daily progress in detail, including urine output and food intake, as I felt that these things demonstrated his rapid decline. The nurse unit manager agreed that the patient was in a much worse condition than she had originally thought.

After the meeting, I discussed the situation with my consultant and gave her my opinion that the patient should stay in the unit on compassionate grounds, and she agreed.

Result: The end result was that the patient was able to stay at the unit.

Exceptional answer with full marks:

Situation: I was working in a small hospital in western New South Wales in a unit for patients waiting to be placed in nursing homes or palliative care. An elderly man who had recently been diagnosed with a metastasis to the liver was admitted to our unit while he awaited placement in a nursing home. During his stay, he began rapidly declining and was dying. After a week, the nurse unit manager approached me to say she had phoned a palliative care unit and had found a bed for the elderly man. She said she wanted him transferred as it was costing our unit too much money to have him in a single-stay bed for longer than a week. The patient's son was very, very upset – he was worried the patient would die on the way to the palliative care unit, without dignity and in an unfamiliar environment. I agreed with him.

Task: My goal was to help manage the situation and maintain the patient's dignity.

Action: I requested a meeting with the nurse unit manager and the patient's son to discuss the situation. I brought notes with me and informed the nurse and son of the patient's daily progress. I explained the patient's urine output and food intake, as I felt that these things demonstrated his rapid decline.

I showed empathy to both parties by remaining calm and quiet, and listening to their concerns. I asked the son how he was coping and said to him, "I understand this is a really difficult time for you and the family. Rest assured I'm going to do everything I can to support your father and make sure he has the best care possible."

When I spoke to the nurse unit manager, I said: "I understand you're concerned about the financial impacts of having patients in palliative care and that it can be hard to support them." The nurse unit manager thanked me for listening to her and said she agreed that the patient was in a much worse condition than she had initially thought.

After the meeting, I called my consultant to discuss the situation and gave her my opinion that I thought the patient should stay in the unit on compassionate grounds, and she agreed.

Result: The end result was that the patient was able to stay in the unit. The son thanked me for caring about his father, and the nursing staff also said they were pleased the patient was staying in the unit, as they didn't agree with the nurse unit manager's initial decision to have him moved. I also received positive feedback from my consultant for the way I handled the situation.

I learnt that by acknowledging how others feel, they're more open to discussion and it's easier to arrive at a mutually agreeable decision. I have since mentored students on how to deal with similar situations with their own patients.

Notice the extra detail in the second answer. It provides a more specific account of the actions taken to achieve the goal, and provides an in-depth explanation of how empathy and understanding were shown to both parties. By giving this kind of detail in your answers, you provide the panel with a clear picture of your positive behavioural skills.

Some other examples of behavioural-based questions you can use to prepare for your interview:

Tell us about a time when you …

- Followed something through to completion
- Made a mistake
- Received negative feedback
- Used holistic thinking
- Didn't know how to manage a situation
- Were proactive
- Showed altruistic patient focus
- Dealt with a difficult patient
- Dealt with a difficult family
- Worked with an under-performing colleague

Ethical questions

Ethical questions are another way for the panel to predict your future behaviour. Unlike behaviour-based questions, ethics-based questions focus on hypothetical scenarios.

There are three key elements to structuring your answer to an ethics-based question:

1. **Make a decision.** This may sound obvious, but you need to make a decision about what you would do in the scenario you're presented with, rather than sit on the fence and offer a vague answer. Saying, "Oh, I don't know. I might do this or I might do that, but it depends …" will not win you marks.

2. **Intervention.** What needs to be solved? What action would you take and why? You need to explain who you would help, who you would seek advice from, and who and what would be impacted by your actions (including

yourself, patient, family, colleagues and hospital). What kind of training would you undertake or implement for others?

3. **Prevention.** This is an important point that people often overlook when asked an ethics-based question. How would you prevent the situation from happening again? Would you follow up with all parties involved?

The following model demonstrates how to approach ethics-based questions.

Managing ethics-based questions

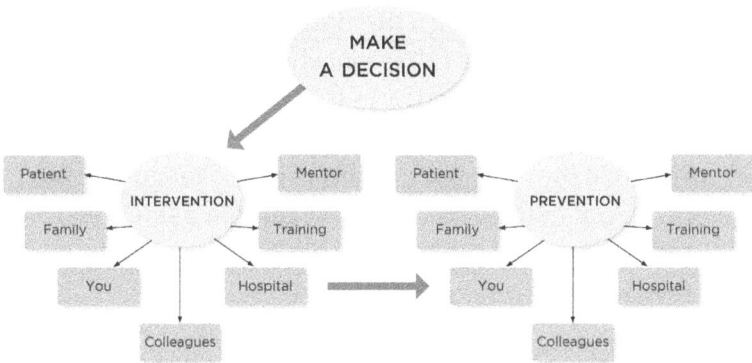

© Jane Anderson 2016

Here are some examples of ethical questions and how to answer them:

Question 1: You are on duty and a patient requires a procedure. Your consultant arrives and is about to perform the operation. You smell alcohol on his

breath and suspect that he is drunk. What would you do?

Decision

I would stop the operation. Patient care is paramount and I have a duty of care to both the patient and my colleague.

Intervention

Patient: I would let the patient know the surgeon was unwell and the operation would have to be rescheduled.

Family: I would inform the patient's family of the delay. I would also tell them when the operation would likely go ahead.

You: It is my obligation to make my colleague aware of his unfit state. I would try to remain calm and tactful, so as not to put a strain on our working relationship.

Colleague: I would approach my colleague in a professional, non-judgemental and tactful manner by remaining calm and talking to them in private. I would determine whether the consultant really was drunk, or whether he was simply unwell. If I he was drunk, I would express my strong concern about him doing the operation. I would remind him that he had a duty of care – both moral and medicolegal – to the patient, and emphasise that he would be putting his career at risk if he decided to do the surgery.

Ultimately, I would not allow the surgeon to operate. I would also ensure he got home safely.

Hospital: I would bring an anaesthetist and orthopaedic consultant into the situation, and talk to the head of department.

Mentor: For reassurance on how to proceed, I would contact one of my trusted superiors.

Prevention

Patient: I would follow up with the patient to check if they were OK and reassure them their procedure would take place shortly.

Family: I would ask the patient if they would like me to keep the family updated on the situation and reassure them that the hospital was working on rescheduling the surgery.

You: I would take the time to reflect on how I handled the situation and whether I should have done anything differently.

Colleague: I would follow up with my colleague over a coffee to find out how he was going. If during our conversation it became clear that he had an ongoing problem with alcohol, I would gently encourage him to seek professional support, such as from an EAP provider or psychologist.

Hospital: I would find out if the policy on how to deal with a staff member under the influence of alcohol was up to date. I would also find out whether other staff had encountered similar situations. If there was any indication that working while drunk was a cultural issue, I would consider pursuing the issue further.

Mentor: I would discuss the approach I took with my mentor and seek their advice on whether I should have handled the situation differently.

Training: I would consider how I could use this experience as an example when teaching other students, so that they would be armed with information if they ever found themselves in a similar situation with a colleague.

Question 2: You're on shift and an intern makes a mistake, giving a patient an overdose of Warfarin. What do you do?

Decision

Patient care is the priority and I must reduce harm to the patient.

Intervention

Patient: I would review the patient and identify any evidence of harm. I would let the patient know what was being done to prevent it happening again.

Family: If the overdose had harmed the patient, I would inform the family.

You: I would remain calm and focused to keep the

situation under control. I would consult a specialist for advice on how to proceed with the patient.

Colleague: I would make the intern aware of what had happened by having a professional, non-aggressive and non-threatening conversation with them in private. I would ask them if they were aware that they had administered an overdose, and offer advice in a constructive and helpful manner.

Hospital: I would make a note on the patient's chart so other staff would know not to issue any more medication.

Mentor: I would seek advice from a trusted mentor on what other steps I should take with the patient and intern.

Training: If the intern needed further training, I would offer to train them myself or take steps to find the appropriate training for them.

Prevention

Patient: I would regularly check in on the patient to see if they were OK and address any concerns they had. I would reassure them that the intern was undergoing further training and steps were being taken to ensure it would not happen again.

Family: I would keep the family updated on the patient's condition and reassure them that extra training was being implemented.

You: I would reflect on whether there was something I could have done to prevent the intern from administering an overdose. I might need to pay closer attention to them when administering medication.

Colleague: I would follow up with the intern to find out how their training was going to determine whether the learning gap had been bridged.

Hospital: I would talk to my superiors to discuss the possibility of reviewing the hospital's policy on interns administering medication.

Mentor: I would follow up with my mentor to get advice on whether I had handled the situation adequately.

Training: I would suggest to the hospital that all interns undergo extra training in administering medication.

Question 3: After having a back operation, a patient complains that their pain is worse than before. They ask you for advice about suing the operating surgeon. What would you do?

Decision

I must take any complaint from a patient seriously. Effective communication with the patient and surgeon is paramount so a fair outcome can be achieved for both parties.

Intervention

Patient: In a quiet, private room, I would respectfully listen to the patient's concerns and try to define their exact problem. I would obtain a thorough history and examination, and review the patient's notes, operative report and radiographs. I would explain to the patient that complications can occur and there are multiple reasons why. I would emphasise that I could not pass judgment on the surgeon, as I was not present during the operation. I would also discuss with the patient their recovery and rehabilitation, and organise a follow-up plan that includes regular assessment of their condition.

Family: I would ask the patient if they would like me to explain the situation to their family. I would let the family know the hospital was taking steps to address the issue.

You: I would remain respectful of both parties and refrain from jumping to conclusions.

Colleague: I would notify the surgeon of the patient's concerns in a non-confrontational, professional and tactful manner, and ask them for their view of the situation.

Hospital: I would notify my superiors and seek advice on what kind of assistance to give to the patient. They may tell me that the situation should be handled by someone other than myself.

Mentor: I would seek guidance from a trusted mentor on how to proceed. I would ask them whether I should give the patient further advice or refer them to someone with more legal knowledge than myself.

Training: I would research what would happen if the patient did decide to pursue legal action. I would also read any hospital policies on such matters.

Prevention

Patient: I would keep in touch with the patient to reassure them that the hospital was taking their concerns seriously and was investigating the matter.

Family: I would make myself available to the patient's family if they had any concerns with how matters were proceeding. I would also update them on the patient's physical recovery.

You: I would reflect on whether I handled the situation adequately.

Colleague: I would keep in touch with my colleague and offer them my support.

Hospital: I would talk to other staff members to determine whether the situation was a common one, and if it was, I would follow it up with my superiors to see if something could be done about it.

Mentor: I would seek advice from a superior on how I handled the situation, and whether I could have done things differently.

Training: I would familiarise myself with any hospital policies in relation to patients wanting to take legal action against the staff and hospital.

Psychometric questions

Some of the more competitive specialties now use psychometric profiling tools during medical interviews. When a panel is faced with an enormous pool of talent to choose from, psychometric testing can help it select only the very best people for a training program.

Hogan Personality Inventory

The Hogan Personality Inventory (HPI) is a psychometric tool widely used for recruitment purposes. It is also commonly used by specialty interview panels to predict job performance. The HPI assesses personal characteristics, noting strengths and weaknesses, to aid decisions about recruitment and professional development. It involves 206 true-or-false questions and takes about 15-20 minutes to complete.

The seven primary scales of the HPI and their interpretations are as follows:

- **Adjustment:** Confidence, self-esteem and composure under pressure.
  - o High score: Confident, resilient and optimistic.
  - o Low score: Tense, irritable and negative.

- **Ambition:** Initiative, competitiveness and a desire for leadership roles.
  - o High score: Competitive and eager to advance.

- o Low score: Unassertive and less interested in advancement.

- **Sociability:** Extroversion, gregarious and need for social interaction.
  - o High score: Outgoing, colourful, impulsive and dislikes working alone.
  - o Low score: Reserved, quiet and prefers working alone.

- **Interpersonal sensitivity:** Tact, perceptiveness and ability to maintain relationships.
  - o High score: Friendly, warm and popular.
  - o Low score: Independent, frank and direct.

- **Prudence:** Self-discipline, responsibility and conscientiousness.
  - o High score: Organised, dependable and thorough.
  - o Low score: Impulsive, flexible and creative.

- **Inquisitive:** Imagination, curiosity and creative potential.
  - o High score: Quick witted, visionary and pays less attention to details.
  - o Low score: Practical, focused and able to concentrate for long periods.

- **Learning approach:** Achievement-oriented and up-to-date on business and technical matters.
  - o High score: Enjoys reading and studying.
  - o Low score: More interested in hands-on learning than formal education.

The panel makes links between your HPI scores and the competencies of your specialty. It may even seek advice from a recruiting firm. The panel may also use your HPI scores to specifically tailor questions for you. Take, for example, the scale of interpersonal sensitivity, which is about maintaining relationships. If you received a high score, the panel might ask you to describe how you would manage and overcome team conflict. The panel might also ask you what you would do if you disagreed with a colleague's treatment of a patient. If you received a low interpersonal sensitivity score, the panel might ask you these same questions, but with a view to determining whether you could overcome your lack of tact and social perceptiveness.

You can prepare yourself for this kind of questioning by looking at the HPI scales and rating yourself. Ask yourself:

- Would you get a low score on any of the scales?
- How have you managed these weaknesses in the past?
- What scales would you score highly on?
- How do these high scores relate to your competencies?

CHAPTER 7
PRACTICE

"Knowledge is of no value unless you put it into practice."
– Anton Chekhov

Now that you've done all the groundwork – you understand your competencies and you have prepared your answers to the panel's questions – it is time to reinforce your self-selling training through *practice*. As a doctor, you have an extremely tight schedule. It is important you get the best-possible return on investment for the time you spend practising for your panel interview.

Think of it as running a marathon. You can't just wake up one day and decide that you're going to run 42.2 kilometres. You not only need to train for months in advance, you need to train *well*. Each training session must have a goal (e.g. speed, hills, long run) and you need to schedule them into your week, otherwise life gets in the way and you won't log all the kilometres you need, making it harder for you to finish the race.

Similarly, you need to schedule into your week your interview practice sessions, each with a specific goal, so you can walk into your interview confident and ready to sell yourself to the panel.

I once had a client who worked obsessively in the few months leading to his interview. His work schedule was tight and hectic, and included a stint overseas. This made it incredibly difficult for him to practise for his interview. It's important you don't leave practising to the last minute. It may feel repetitive, and that's OK. The repetition helps strengthen your ability to sell yourself to the panel. As Chinese political and military leader Chiang Kai-shek said in 1939, "The more you sweat in peace, the less you bleed in war."

When should I start practising?

Don't underestimate how much time you will need to practise. I don't recommend you leave it any less than two months prior to your panel interview. I even have clients who work with me a year in advance.

Having said that, professional coaching will help you reduce the amount of time you need to prepare well. In just one two-hour coaching session, I can help clients reduce their preparation by days, simply by helping them plan their interview practice schedule.

Practice schedule

A practice schedule ensures you allocate enough time to create and strengthen your neural pathways for a successful interview. It also helps keep your stress levels under control so you feel calm and able to cope under pressure.

The following guide will help you create a practice schedule. It is based over the two-month period leading up to your interview, but you may want to schedule your sessions over a longer time frame.

PRACTICE SCHEDULE

TWO MONTHS PRIOR

- Create your answers to the Magic Five Questions. Write them down, read them aloud and time yourself.
- If your timing falls short, add more content and ensure it links to the competencies.
- If you're speaking for too long, focus on being more succinct.

TWO WEEKS PRIOR

- Continue to practise your answers aloud and ensure your timing is correct.
- Decide what to wear to your interview.
- You can start to introduce other past or practice answers into your schedule to improve your confidence and agility.

ONE WEEK PRIOR

- Try on the clothes you have chosen to wear to your interview to make sure they fit and feel comfortable.
- Again, practice your answers out loud and prepare past questions.

THREE DAYS PRIOR

- Get a friend or colleague to ask you a selection of questions so you can rehearse your answers under pressure.

ONE DAY PRIOR

- Eat well and stay hydrated.
- Practise slow, regulated breathing and read over your answers.
- Turn your phone off or give it to a relative or friend to look after so you can focus and centre yourself for the next day.
- Arrive at your hotel and identify exactly where you need to go for your interview to avoid last-minute stress.
- Organise or book any transport you need to get to your interview to reduce the amount of decisions that need to be made on the day.

Practising involves more than verbally rehearsing your answers. Non-verbal communication plays a vital role during your interview. You need to master effective body language to have maximum impact on the panel and get top marks.

Body language

The panel makes unconscious decisions about you based on your body language. You may think, "But isn't what I say during my interview what matters?" Yes, it does matter, but the way you physically compose yourself – your posture, hand gestures, facial expressions and tone of voice – impacts the panellists' judgements, whether they realise it or not. Body language not only influences how others perceive you – it affects your own thought patterns, too.

There are five key elements to effective body language:

1. Dress well
2. Posture
3. Eye contact
4. Smile
5. Be confident, not arrogant

Dress well

> *"Shoes transform your body language and attitude.*
> *They lift you physically and emotionally."*
> *– Christian Louboutin*

To make a good impression, you need to dress well for your interview. It creates a halo effect: when you dress well, the panel is more likely to view you in a positive light.

This impact of dress is highlighted by research conducted by Frank Bernieri, an associate professor of psychology at Oregon State University. In his study, Bernieri found that most interviewers decided within the first 10 seconds of meeting a candidate whether they were the right person for the job or not. Job seekers who dressed conservatively for their interview were more likely to be hired than those who looked less polished.

Carefully choosing your attire demonstrates to the panel that you have put thought and effort into your interview. It also shows the panellists that you respect them, which in turn builds build their trust in you.

I once had a client called Peter, who wanted to get into periodontics. He arrived for one of our practice interviews wearing a pinstripe suit. Periodontists frequently deal with patients who are nervous and fearful of experiencing pain during their dental procedures. Building trust is paramount if the periodontist is to see them again. Peter's suit, while beautiful, made him look like a gangster – not the kind of look you want when you need to build trust!

The key to dressing well for your interview is to be conservative. Avoid black, as it has negative connotations. Instead, choose navy, charcoal or grey, as these are strong trust colours. Gents, you need to wear a suit. Nothing over the top, but I suggest you wear a tie. Choose a tie colour that matches your eyes. It will brighten your appearance and help the panel connect with you more easily.

Ladies, I suggest you wear a suit or below-the-knee skirt. Ensure your shoes are matte, not patent or shiny, and wear skin-coloured stockings. Black stockings look too heavy and do not complement a dark-coloured skirt or suit. Tie your hair back so that it is off your face, ensuring you appear refreshed and alert. Wear minimal jewellery: one ring, one necklace and a pair of earrings should be the maximum.

You also want to feel comfortable in your attire, so try on your outfit the week before your interview to ensure it fits well. You don't want to be fidgeting with your clothes in front of the panel!

Posture

"Human beings are natural mimickers. The more you're conscious of the other side's posture, mannerisms and word choices – and the more you subtly reflect those back – the more accurate you'll be at taking their perspective."
– Dan Pink

Posture is a critical component of non-verbal communication. It affects how others perceive you, and also how you perceive yourself. A strong posture will not only boost the panel's confidence about you and your abilities, it will enhance your confidence, too.

Research conducted by the University of Northern Iowa College of Business Administration indicates that people with an "open" posture are perceived as more persuasive than those with a "closed" posture. An open posture conveys friendliness and trustworthiness, while a closed posture – arms crossed over chest, body hunched forward and turned away from the audience – gives the impression of detachment and hostility. To maintain an open posture, ensure your hands are faced outwards, sit or stand straight with your head raised, relax your facial expression and maintain eye contact.

For more information on good posture and body language, I recommend you watch the TED talk by Amy Cuddy, professor and researcher at Harvard Business School. Cuddy reveals how body position – "power posing" – influences others, and even your own brain. She offers a number of two-minute power poses that will help you improve your posture and get you into the mindset of someone who is confident and successful.

You can also work on your seated posture by using an old newsreader trick. Put one thumb on your bellybutton and the other on the middle of your chest. Push your top thumb upward, as though you are drawing your spine up, so you sit straight in your chair.

In the minutes before your interview, rather than waiting with the other candidates and sitting with a closed posture, I recommend you step outside or into the bathroom and take a few moments to practice your open posture. It will help change your mindset so that you are confident and psychologically ready for your interview.

Eye contact

Eye contact helps you connect with your audience. Looking at the panel directly, without glaring at them, gives you an aura of honesty and confidence, ensuring your answers have stronger impact so you get more marks.

The importance of eye contact was demonstrated by a group of Cornell researchers, who examined how eye contact can influence feelings of trust and connections with a brand. In their study, participants were randomly shown one of two versions of a cereal box. Both versions displayed an image of a "spokes-character" rabbit, but on one box the rabbit looked straight ahead at the viewer, while on the other the rabbit's gaze was turned downwards and away from the viewer. The researchers found that the participants' trust in the cereal brand was 16% higher and their *connection* to the brand was 28% higher when they viewed the spokes-character rabbit that made direct eye contact.

If the panellists are busy writing and not looking at you, try to stay focused on them so that when they do look up, you can connect with them. Take the time to acknowledge all of the panellists by making eye contact with each one during your interview. The amount of eye contact you make will diminish when you access internal thoughts and memories – you may look to the ceiling or to your side while giving an answer, and that's fine. You don't have to have eye contact with the panel 100% of the time – a good benchmark is 50%.

Practising your answers will naturally help you improve your eye contact. Knowing what you will say and feeling confident about your answers mean it's less likely you will fumble for answers, losing focus and eye contact, during your interview.

Smile

> *"We shall never know all the good that a simple smile can do."*
> *– Mother Teresa*

A smile is essential to connecting with others. Smiling not only helps you engage with the panel; it is a fundamental indication that you meet the competency of interpersonal skills. The panel needs to gauge your ability to communicate and interact effectively with patients and colleagues. Smiling is an important part of this process.

If the panel is not smiling at you, don't be disconcerted. Your smile will not go unnoticed; it will influence the panel on an unconscious level, as well as on a conscious level as they mark you on your social skills.

A smile is like an amplifier: it helps your message resonate with your audience. It's also healthy for you! Smiling reduces stress-inducing hormones, such as cortisol and adrenaline, and increases mood-enhancing hormones, such as endorphins.

Ron Gutman, public speaker and founder of HealthTap, gave an interesting TED talk on the hidden power of a smile. He reviewed a range of studies on smiling, including evidence that your smile can be a predictor of your lifespan. Researchers from Wayne State University conducted a study in 2010 that examined baseball cards featuring headshots of Major League players in 1952. The study found that the players who had smiled in their photos had lived longer than the players who did not smile. The players who smiled lived an average of 79.9 years, while those who didn't lived an average of 72.9 years. Interestingly, Gutman also revealed that 30% of people smile more than 20 times a day, 14% smile less than five times a day, and children smile as many as 400 times a day!

Smiling is contagious. It encourages others to feel happy and it helps your confidence grow. Practise smiling as you rehearse your answers in front of a mirror. If you are a more serious type, you will soon find smiling will come more naturally. You'll look and feel more enthusiastic, you'll articulate your answers competently, and you will walk into your interview able to connect with the panel.

Be confident, not arrogant

The panel wants to select only the very best candidates for their specialty program. Your self-confidence helps the panellists feel at ease and builds their trust in your abilities. Arrogance, on the other hand, makes others feel uncomfortable and nervous. In a medical situation, arrogance is potentially dangerous. It could lead to incorrect and harmful decisions. It is difficult for the panel to trust you if you come across as arrogant.

For example, I worked with a client called Andrew who was trying to get into his chosen specialty program. He was friendly but cocky. He came from a family of medical experts and I got the sense from him that he thought he knew everything. My feedback to him was: "You're obviously very talented and you know what you're doing, but the impression you give is a little arrogant. You come across as over confident. You risk making the panel feel nervous – they might think you would be too proud to ask for help when you needed it. In fact, you might not even be aware when you don't know something because your pride could get in the way."

Andrew did not get into his program that year. However, he came back to me the following year and was far more humble. He was still highly confident, but the cockiness had disappeared. He was more compassionate and present, and that year he was so successful during his interview that he got on to his chosen program.

Confidence and arrogance can be likened to a magnet. Confidence attracts while arrogance repels. As Brené Brown, American scholar and public speaker, said: "When you lose your capacity to care what other people think, you've lost your ability to connect." In your interview, your job is to connect with the panel by caring about what they think and attracting them to you.

To avoid appearing arrogant during your interview, **you should not**:

- Arrive late.
- Make intimidating movements, such strutting into the room, slouching, finger pointing and putting your hands on your hips.
- Avoid eye contact.
- Interrupt the panellists when they speak.
- Pretend you have an answer for everything. Don't be afraid to admit to your mistakes. It is an opportunity for you to show the panel how you have overcome and learned from them.

Managing nerves

Feeling nervous before and during your interview is normal. A small amount of nervousness helps you stay alert and focused. However, you need to keep your stress levels under control during your interview so you can think clearly and creatively. If you are too stressed, you will struggle to find the right words and say too much or too little. Your heart rate will rise and you will start to feel panicky. Your brain will go into cognitive overload and you'll wish you were somewhere else.

Melissa was a client of mine who particularly struggled with anxiety and nerves. Most of my clients book four sessions with me in the lead-up to their specialty interview. Melissa booked eight. She was so anxious and stressed that her heart rate went into overdrive even outside our coaching sessions. Melissa was a perfectionist, which added to the pressure she felt. For five of her eight sessions, we worked on the content of her answers. For the remaining three sessions, we worked on lowering her heart rate. I hooked Melissa up to a heart-rate monitor so we could see exactly how high her heart rate was. We took steps to lower it and, before long, Melissa had her heart rate completely under control. She was markedly calmer and, as a result, she blitzed her interview and achieved her place on the dermatology program.

To remain calm during your interview, your brain needs to get enough oxygen. A nifty free app called MyCalmBeat (available on iTunes and Google Play) teaches you how to improve your calmness and resilience through slow breathing. It calculates your personal best breathing rate and then gives you tools to train yourself to breathe at that frequency. I know many people, from public speakers to athletes, who use MyCalmBeat to help them cope with high-pressure situations.

Being interrupted

One of the most off-putting experiences during your interview is when you are cut off by the panel. You could be in the middle of answering a question when you are brusquely told: "Thank you, that's enough. We're ready to go on to the next question now."

Being interrupted by the panel can feel as though you've just walked into a glass door: you didn't see it coming and it disorients you. You lose your momentum and train of thought. The key is to not take it personally. Be prepared for it; the panel could be testing you to see how you cope under pressure.

One of my clients, Sarah, suffered greatly when she was interrupted during her medical interview. Whenever she was cut off by the panel, her confidence plummeted: she believed their interruptions indicated they didn't want to hear what she had to say. She berated herself that what she had been saying was incorrect. In fact, the opposite was true: what Sarah had been saying was exactly what the panel had wanted to hear. The panel had simply received enough information from her answer and was ready to move to the next question. After some coaching sessions with me, Sarah's confidence rapidly improved. She was able to prepare for her next interview more effectively, and was delighted to get on to her chosen specialty training program.

Being interrupted feels uncomfortable, but it's important you don't dwell on it. Before your interview, practise your answers with a friend or colleague with the prior instruction that they cut you off at some point. This will help you learn how to stop, re-focus and be prepared for the next question.

CHAPTER 8

ON THE DAY

Feeling a bit nervous on the day of your panel interview is perfectly normal. After all, you've been working towards this day for a long time! They key is to not let your nerves get the better of you. By now, you know your competencies, you know what to expect during your interview, and you are armed with the skills and techniques to successfully sell yourself to the panel.

It's important you stay in a positive and confident frame of mind on interview day by taking care of a few practicalities. Plan ahead as much as possible and don't leave anything until the last minute. This will ensure the day goes as smoothly as possible for you.

What to take to your interview

There are some essential items you need to take to your interview. They will give you a reference point and help you focus on what you need to say. They will also provide the panellists with further information and demonstrate to them that you are thoroughly prepared for the interview.

You should bring:

- Your resume
- Details of two to three referees
- Your portfolio, including examples of your work (such

as research and papers you have had published), written references and certificates
- A print-out of the company website
- A list of questions to ask the panel (suggested questions are provided at the end of this chapter)

Eat and drink well

Try not to arrive at your interview on an empty stomach. If you're feeling nervous, you may feel as though you'd rather not eat – but to stay focused and maintain mental clarity, it is important you fuel your body with healthy food. Avoid too much caffeine, and do not drink alcohol the night before.

It is also important that you stay well hydrated. Nervousness can give you a dry mouth, which makes speaking difficult. Drink plenty of water the day before and on the morning of your interview.

Cut the distractions

To stay focused, you need to minimise distractions. Turn off your mobile phone or have calls diverted in the hour or two leading up to your interview – and especially during your interview! It is extremely off-putting for both you and the panel if your phone rings or beeps while the interview is in progress.

Steer clear of social media before your interview. There are far too many opportunities for distraction on Facebook, Twitter and other social media sites.

Arrive well ahead of time

Arrive at the place of your interview 30 minutes early. It is much more desirable to arrive too early than too late. If you leave too late, you're likely to feel flustered and stressed that you won't arrive on time. These feelings can flow over into your interview, with potentially disastrous results.

Ideally, you should organise your transport to the venue a day or more in advance. Make sure you book a taxi or organise with a friend or relative to drive you to the venue, so you can keep your mind on the task ahead without having to worry about traffic.

Don't let others put you off

Seeing the other candidates while you wait for your interview can sometimes make your confidence falter. If the other candidates seem older than you, you may think that they must have more experience and are more qualified than you. This is not necessarily so.

Don't let the other candidates put you off your game. Remember, you are a highly experienced doctor who has put in the hard yards with your interview preparations, and you have as much right to your training program as the other candidates.

Get into 'the zone'

While you wait for your interview, spend the time channelling the calm and in-control state of mind you need to be in. Practise your slow-breathing techniques and quietly read over your answers.

Practise good posture. Avoid slouching, standing with your hands on your hips or sitting huddled together with the other candidates, as these postures elicit negative emotions. Adopting an open posture before your interview will encourage you to maintain it in front of the panel.

During your interview

Remember to maintain eye contact with the panellists and continue your open posture. Sit facing the panel with your head raised and facial expression relaxed. Speak clearly and concisely, and don't be afraid to ask the panellists to repeat a question if you did not hear it clearly.

Be courteous and respectful. Shake the panellists' hands if it is appropriate and if there is time.

Questions for the panel

The following is a list of suggested questions you could ask the panel. Asking questions will not only give you more of an insight into the specialty training program, it shows the panel you are genuinely interested in the specialty and determined to achieve your place on the program.

- Can you describe this school's curriculum in the pre-clinical and clinical years? Are there any innovations, such as problem-based learning?
- Are there opportunities for students to design, conduct and publish their own research?
- Is there flexibility in the coursework (the number of electives) and the timing of the courses?
- Has this medical school, or any of its clinical

departments, been on probation or had its accreditation revoked?

- How do students from this medical school perform on the National Board Examinations?
- How are students evaluated academically? How are clinical evaluations performed?
- Is there a formal mechanism in place for students to evaluate their professors and attending physicians? What changes have been made recently as a result of this feedback?
- What kind of academic, personal, financial and career counselling is available to students? Are these services also offered to their spouses and dependents/children?
- Is there a mentor/adviser system? Who are the advisers — faculty members, other students, or both?
- How diverse is the student body? Are there support services or organisations available for ethnic minorities and women?
- Can you tell me about the library and extracurricular facilities (i.e. housing and athletic/recreational facilities)?
- Are there computer facilities available to students? Are they integrated into the curriculum/learning?
- What type of clinical sites — ambulatory, private preceptors, private hospitals, rural settings — are available or required for clerkships? Does this school allow for students to do rotations at other institutions or internationally?
- Is a car necessary for clinical rotations? Is parking a problem?
- Are there stable levels of federal financial aid and substantial amounts of university/medical school endowment aid available to students?
- Is someone available to assist students with budgeting and financial planning?

- What medical school committees (e.g. curriculum committee) have student representation?
- Are students involved in (required or voluntary) community service?
- How active is the student council/government? Are there other student organisations?
- Is there an established protocol for dealing with student exposure to infectious diseases?
- Is disability insurance provided to cover this exposure?
- Does this school provide, or does the student pay for, vaccinations against Hepatitis B or prophylactic AZT treatment in case of a needle-stick or accident?
- Is there a school honour code? Is there a grievance process or procedure? Are the students involved?
- May I see a list of residency programs that this school's recent graduates were accepted into?
- Does this school have strengths in the type of medicine (primary versus specialised care, urban versus rural practice environment, academic medicine versus private practice) I will want to practice?
- Do you have any concerns about me being on the training program?

Final word

After reading this book, you are now equipped with all the tools you need for effective interview preparation. You know what steps to take to confidently sell yourself to the panel – and you can do it! I wish you all the very best with your medical specialty training interview.

If you would like further coaching with me, please contact me at jane@jane-anderson.com.au.

APPENDIX

PRACTICE QUESTIONS

The following is a selection of panel interview questions you can use during your interview preparations. Use them to formulate your answers and to practise your self-selling techniques. These questions relate to the specialties of:

- Cardiology
- Dermatology
- General surgery
- Geriatrics
- Obstetrics and gynaecology
- Urology

There is also a set of **general** questions that could be asked during any specialty interview.

Cardiology

- What are the positional changes in pain noted by patients with pericarditis?
- How long does it take for total CPK levels in the blood to return to normal after a myocardial infarction?
- What is the kussmaul sign?
- What is the most specific and sensitive indicator for re-myocardial infarction (RE-MI)?
- Describe the classical signs of mitral stenosis.
- Who performed the first open-heart surgery: Daniel Hale Williams or Ludwig Rehn?

- What is peripheral resistance?
- What was the surgical method for the first open-heart surgery?
- What are the most common causes of cardiovascular-related syncope?
- How often does rupture of the pulmonary artery occur with the right heart catheterisation?
- What is the effect of inspiration of the return of venous blood to the heart?
- What are the electrocardiogram findings of a Mobitz type II second-degree AV block?
- How often will the EKG be abnormal in patients having an MI?
- Normal JVD is 6cm-8cm. What five conditions are associated with increased JVD?
- What are the reversible causes of pulseless electrical activity?
- What are the six Hs?
- What are the six Ts?

Dermatology

- When did you first become interested in dermatology and what have you done to get to this point?
- Give us an example of when you had to deal with conflict. What was the situation? What did you do to resolve it? What was the outcome?
- Give us an example of when you had to put in extra work to achieve a task.
- Give us an example of when you persisted with something because you thought it was right.

General surgery

- What have you done to prepare for surgical training?
- What makes a good leader?
- What attributes make a good general surgeon?
- Can you explain some ways surgeons can assess their own practice?
- What attributes do you possess that will contribute to general surgery?
- What are your weaknesses?
- **Scenario 1:** You have an operation booked for tomorrow and your colleague plans to do the operation differently to you. How do you resolve this difference?
- **Scenario 2:** You have a resident that the nurse unit manager says is not performing well. How do you deal with this?
- **Scenario 3:** Your boss turns up for an emergency laparotomy and it's apparent he's intoxicated. How do you deal with this?
- **Scenario 4:** You are in outpatients with your consultant and another consultant calls to ask you to help him in theatre. Your own consultant refuses to let you leave, saying that you have to finish your clinic. There is no one else available to help in clinic or OT. How do you manage the situation? What do you do from here?
- **Scenario 5:** You have a resident who is not performing adequately – leaving early, not following up tests, etc. Your other resident is working hard and picking up the slack. How do you deal with this situation?

Geriatrics

- What training do you think you should have to undertake to become a consultant geriatrician?
- When and why did you decide to become a geriatrician?
- Why did you want to concentrate on stroke medicine?
- What qualities make a good consultant geriatrician?
- How would you develop the stroke service?
- What do you think of payment by results in geriatric medicine?
- What is the future for geriatric medicine?
- How would you define quality in geriatrics?
- What is the most important advance in geriatric medicine in the past 10 years?
- What do you think about the super-specialisation of geriatrics?
- What are the three main take-home messages regarding geriatrics that you would want to pass on to undergraduates?
- What is the role of a consultant geriatrician as a manager?
- What is the place of palliative care in geriatric medicine?
- Who should manage a patient with a stroke?

Obstetrics and gynaecology

- How does RANZCOG ensure you are a competent specialist after you complete training?
- Discuss a health issue affecting your community and strategies to improve it.
- **Scenario 1:** You are in a rural area for six months and the maternal and perinatal mortality rate is double the national average. How do you improve this?

- **Scenario 2:** A 34-week pregnant woman comes to your clinic with her children and one of them tells you she's called Lifeline. What do you do?
- **Scenario 3:** A consultant is concerned about your surgical skills (you are three months into your training). What do you do?

Urology

- What does a urologist do? How do you know? What experience have you had?
- How have you prepared for a career as a urology trainee?
- What do you think might be some issues facing urology over the next five to 10 years?
- What are some ways in which surgeons can assess their own practice?
- **Scenario 1:** You are doing a radical nephrectomy on a Jehovah's Witness, who has specifically stated he does not want any blood products under any circumstances. The operation is complicated and there is damage to IVC with significant blood loss. Towards the end, you look up and the anaesthetist has a bag of packed cells running. What are the issues here and how should you manage this situation?
- **Scenario 2:** A father brings his nine-year-old boy in, requesting a circumcision for cultural reasons. You speak to the boy alone and find that he doesn't want an operation. How do you deal with this situation and what are the issues?
- **Scenario 3:** A 40-year-old man presents requesting a vasectomy. You take an informed consent. The man's wife calls you and states that she does not want him to have a vasectomy. She wants to have more children. What

do you understand by informed consent? How do you deal with this situation?

General

Administrative

- Take us through your CV – the highlights and strong points.
- Do you have any changes to make to your resume?
- Have you enrolled in any courses that you plan to attend?
- How many other training programs have you previously applied for?
- Do you have any other applications in at present?

Personal

- Why should we put you on the training program?
- Why do you want to be on the training program?
- What makes you a good fit for the program?
- Where do you see yourself in 10 years' time?
- Why did you become a doctor?
- What is your special interest in this specialty?
- What would you bring to the program?
- What are your strengths/weaknesses?
- What is your biggest fault?
- What makes you angry?
- Describe your personality.
- How do you feel about moving to the area?
- What do you do in your free time?
- What part of the program will be most difficult for you?
- What was your favourite university course and why?
- What do you hope to gain from this experience?

Personal behaviour

- What are the best and worst things that have ever happened to you?
- If your best friends were asked to describe you, what would they say?
- Tell us about a recent triumph/disappointment.
- How do you handle stress?
- Describe how you can effectively deal with someone in crisis.
- Describe your style of communicating and interacting with others.
- Tell us about a time when you demonstrated initiative.
- Tell us about a time when you faced a conflict or felt angry with another individual.
- Tell us about a time when you were criticised unfairly.
- Tell us about a time when you failed.
- How do you handle failure?
- Can you give an example of when you have encouraged good team work?
- Tell us about a time when you've been disappointed in a team-mate or fellow group member. What happened? How did you approach the situation?
- Describe a situation in which you have worked with a diverse group of people. What did you learn from that situation?
- How do you handle change?
- How do you go about making important decisions?
- If you could start your career all over again, what would you do differently?
- If you had the choice of giving a transplant to a successful, elderly member of the community or a 20-year-old drug addict, how would you choose?

Training

- How does your previous training support you for this specialty program?
- Take us through your training so far.
- Why did you do a BSc, MSc? How has it helped you in your working life?
- Do you see any deficiencies in your training?
- Is there any post you regret not doing as a Principal House Officer (PHO)?
- What courses have you attended recently? Were they useful to you?
- What courses would you like to attend?
- Should hospital consultants have spent some time as GPs?
- Who should provide management training?
- In what way was the management course that you attended useful?
- How would you improve training of specialist registrars?

Politics

- What is clinical governance?
- What is your opinion of our last Health Care Commission report?
- How does foundation status help patients?
- Why is acute medicine busier these days?
- How should we measure consultant productivity?
- What do you think of the mission statement of our trust?
- How would you ration health care?
- Is there any limit to the demand for health care?
- How can we ensure patients from ethnic minorities receive proper access to health care?

- Are junior doctors' hours now too short?
- What do you think of the new consultant contract?
- What is the role of consultants in teaching hospitals?
- Does general medicine exist anymore?
- What do you think about private practice?

Teaching

- What did you last teach to nurses?
- What's wrong with undergraduate education?
- How would you make clinical meetings more appealing?
- What will you present on your first grand round?
- What is the purpose of a college tutor?
- What makes a good educational supervisor?
- How should continuing education for consultants be arranged?
- What is the role of a supervisor for an MD/PhD?

Management

- What are the main roles of a multi-disciplinary team leader?
- What do you know about resource management?
- How should intermediate care services be organised?
- Are day hospitals an expensive luxury?
- What are the advantages of day hospitals?
- If you could change one thing in the NHS, what would it be?
- How would you deal with a 10% cut in your budget?
- How would you pay for a new piece of equipment if no new money was obviously available?
- How would you spend a $50,000 one-off grant?
- What are the components of a complaints procedure?
- What do you know of clinical governance?

- What is the difference between audit and governance?
- What clinical audits have you done?
- Who should appraise you?
- How should revalidation be undertaken?
- What do you think of 360 assessments?
- How would you assess user satisfaction with your service?
- How would you reduce the number of acute admissions?
- How might you cut waiting times in your clinic?
- What is your management style?
- How would you deal with an under-performing colleague?
- How would you deal with a colleague who turned up for work drunk?
- What would you do if you strongly disagreed with a colleague's decision?

Research

- What is the importance of research? What are the personal and professional benefits?
- Do you have any current research interests?
- How is research relevant to clinical medicine?
- Why did you do an MSc?
- Explain your MSc in a few short sentences.
- What have you presented recently at an external meeting?
- What journals do you read?
- Tell us about a recent article that caught your eye.
- How would you pursue your research interests in this job?
- Have you been allocated enough sessions for research in your job plan?
- If you haven't got any research to show after a year, should we reduce your salary?

- Do you feel it is important to have published research as a clinician?
- Why are you not the first author on more research?
- Explain how research differs from audit.

Clinical topics

- What are the current controversies in your field?
- What are the main recent developments?
- What constitutes an acceptable delay in diagnosis?
- In which areas do you need more experience?

Closing questions

- Do you have any questions for us?
- If this job is offered, would you accept this job?

Lightning Source UK Ltd.
Milton Keynes UK
UKHW02f0917250918
329483UK00014B/1748/P

9 780994 267832